PICTO MAZES

FIND 72 HIDDEN ANIMALS!

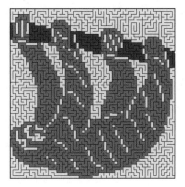

by the Editors at Nikoli Publishing with puzzles by Kazuyuki Yuzawa

Workman Publishing • New York

Copyright © 2018 by Nikoli Co., Ltd.

Library of Congress Cataloging-in-Publication Data is available.

ISBN 978-1-5235-0202-8

Mazes designed by Kazuyuki Yuzawa

Book design by Orlando Adiao

Workman books are available at special discounts when purchased in bulk for premiums and sales promotions as well as for fund-raising or educational use. Special editions or book excerpts can also be created to specification. For details, contact the Special Sales Director at the address below, or send an email to specialmarkets@workman.com.

Workman Publishing Co., Inc.
225 Varick Street
New York, NY 10014-4381

workman.com

WORKMAN is a registered trademark of Workman Publishing Co., Inc.

Printed in China

First printing July 2018

10 9 8 7 6 5 4 3 2 1

Introduction

PictoMazes is a fun new puzzle craze that originated in Japan and has made its way into this book for readers around the world to enjoy. It blends the logic of mazes with the mindfulness of coloring for a unique experience that culminates with a surprising reveal of a hidden picture embedded within the maze. In this book, the hidden images are animals—and, for a bigger challenge, starting on page 95 there may be more than one animal to discover! Read on to learn how to complete each page.

How to Play

Step 1: Use a pencil to solve the maze.
Start your line at one triangular arrow and move toward the second arrow. If you get stuck, try starting at the second arrow and have your lines meet in the middle. *Hint:* Make a special mark when you reach a fork in the road. That way, if you follow the wrong path, it's much easier to backtrack to the split.

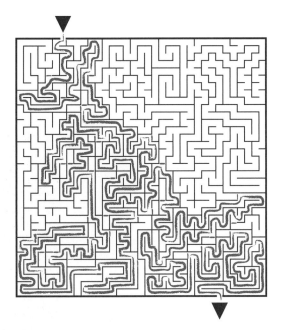

Step 2: Block off the paths not taken.

After you've finished the maze, go along the path and wall off any forks you didn't take. This creates an outline of the hidden picture, and makes the next step marginally easier. Once you've completed a few mazes, you may choose to skip this step and move directly to Step 3.

Step 3: Color the completed maze.

To reveal the picture, use colored pencils to completely shade in the lines along the path you took. Add additional colors as desired in the empty spaces. When you're done, step back and admire the picture!

Their shell can have anywhere
from two to four bands, but out of
the 21 species, only the two three-
banded species can curl into balls.

But *all* species of this particular
animal are capable of other
miraculous physical feats, such
as holding their breath for up to
six minutes. Researchers have
hypothesized that perhaps they
developed this ability to help them
dig burrows. Or perhaps it's because
these armored animals are too heavy
to naturally float. They can choose
to hold their breath and walk across
riverbeds, or they can gulp down
enough air to make themselves
buoyant and float across.

Solution on page 111.

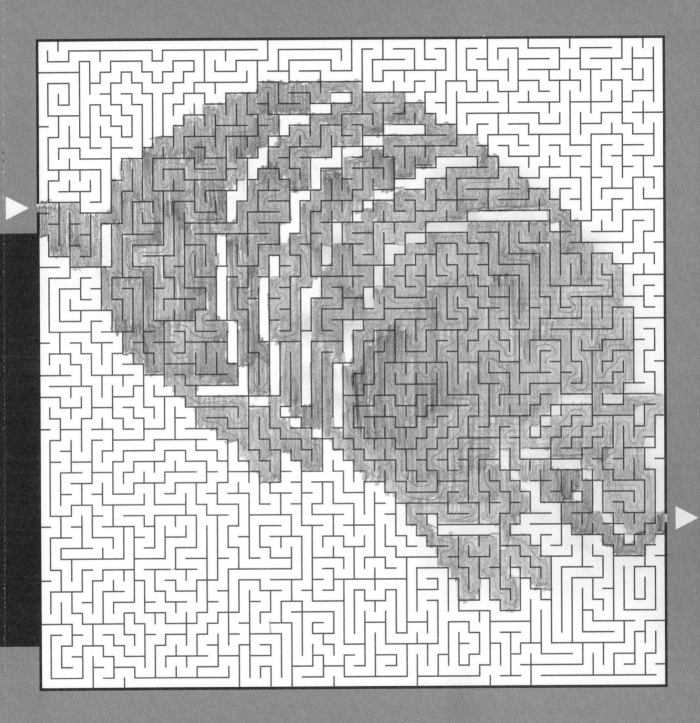

2

This animal isn't the prettiest or most majestic creature, but it *is* fast (it can run up to 34 miles per hour) and smart—not to mention hardy: It can survive for months without water, which is a necessary trait in the grassland region of Africa. Their matriarchal groups, called sounders, create communal dung heaps to confuse predators. It's more difficult to determine the size of the group and if there are any young in the group's care.

Solution on page 111.

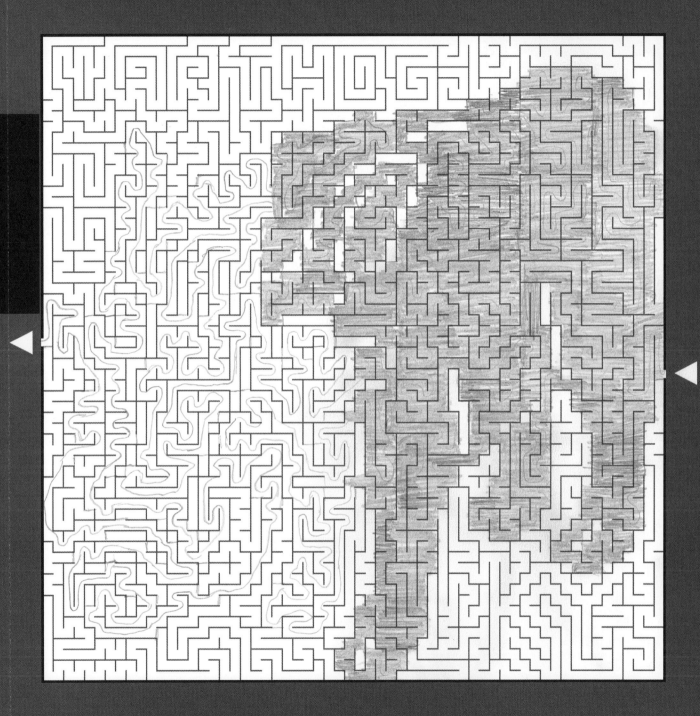

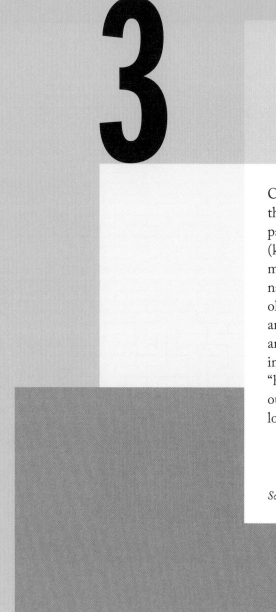

3

Common in Japan, eastern China, the Korean peninsula, Taiwan, and parts of Hawaii, this Japanese bird (known in Japan as the *uguisu*) is much beloved by the people of its native country. Belied by its drab olive and brown color (both male and female), its beautiful voice announces the arrival of spring in its native regions by singing "ho hoke kyo." For food, it seeks out small insects and spiders in low-lying vegetation.

Solution on page 111.

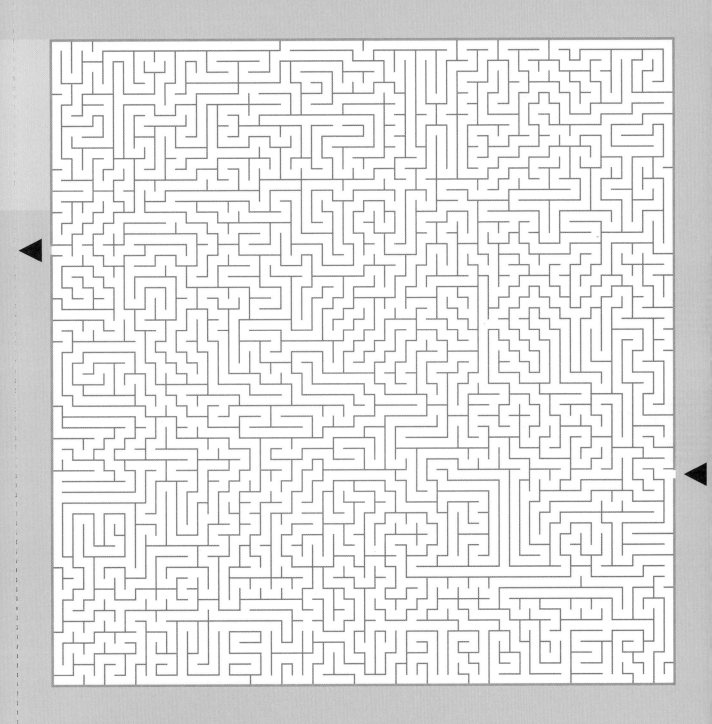

Pterophyllum (part of their scientific name) is derived from the Greek words *pteron* (wing, sail) and *phyllon* (leaf), which describes the graceful shape of this fish's body. Because it is relatively easy to take care of, it is a popular pet. Over the years, this fish has been bred extensively, leading to a wide array of colors and patterns.

Solution on page 111.

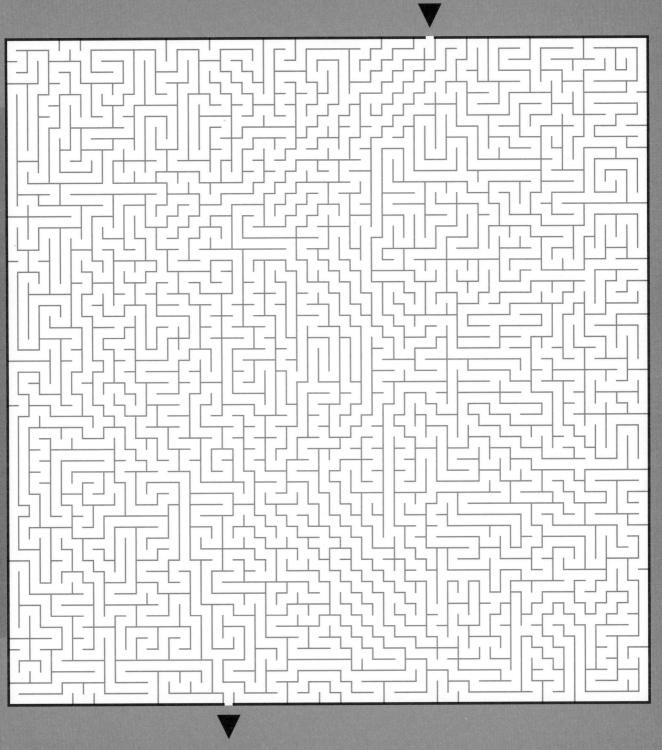

5

This animal is shy, living most of its life alone in the Ituri Rainforest of the Democratic Republic of the Congo. In fact, the species is so elusive that it wasn't discovered by the world at large until 1901.

Giraffes are this animal's closest living relatives, even though the stripes on its legs are reminiscent of zebras'. Like giraffes, they use their long black tongues and stretched necks to eat foliage— 40 to 65 pounds of it every day.

Solution on page 111.

6

Other than its smaller-than-average size, this Seychelles Islands reptile shares quite a few traits with the roughly 200 other species of its kind. This includes the ability to move its eyes independently of each other, change colors, and catch prey with quick strikes of its long tongue.

Perhaps contrary to popular belief, this animal doesn't change color to camouflage itself. Rather, it's a form of communication and a way to regulate its body temperature.

Solution on page 111.

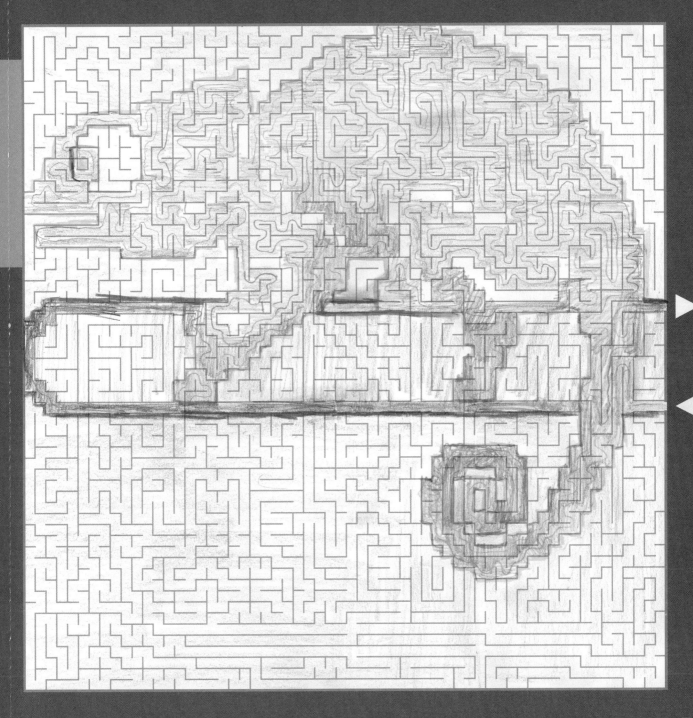

7

These birds are known for pecking at trees to catch insects, make nests, and communicate. They have specific anatomical features that allow them to use their heads in this way, including thicker patches of bone at the front and back of the skull. They peck in short bursts, since friction raises their overall body temperature.

Solution on page 111.

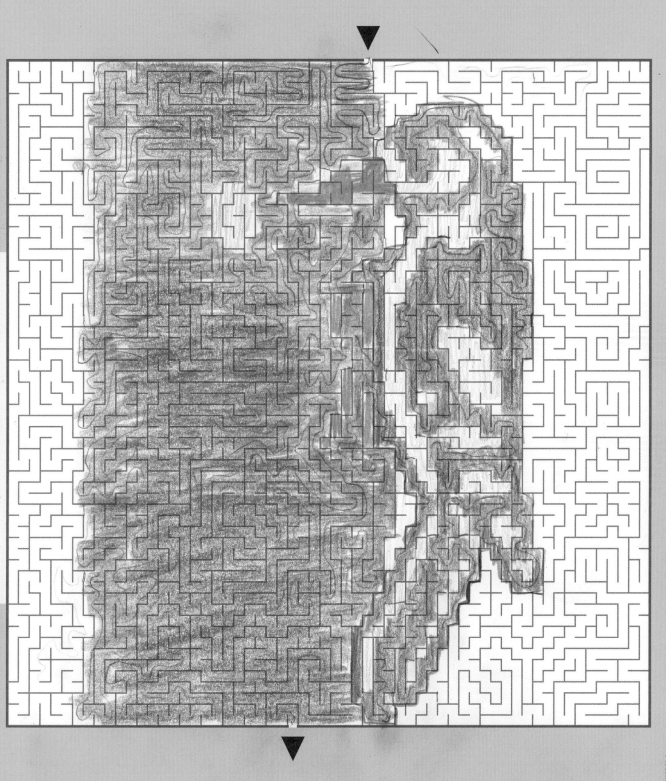

8

These fish are poor swimmers that live in small groups among the stinging tentacles of certain sea anemones. Each fish must build up its immunity to the sting of whatever anemone it calls home. This process takes anywhere from a few minutes to a few hours and has to be repeated if they're away from home for too long.

Solution on page 111.

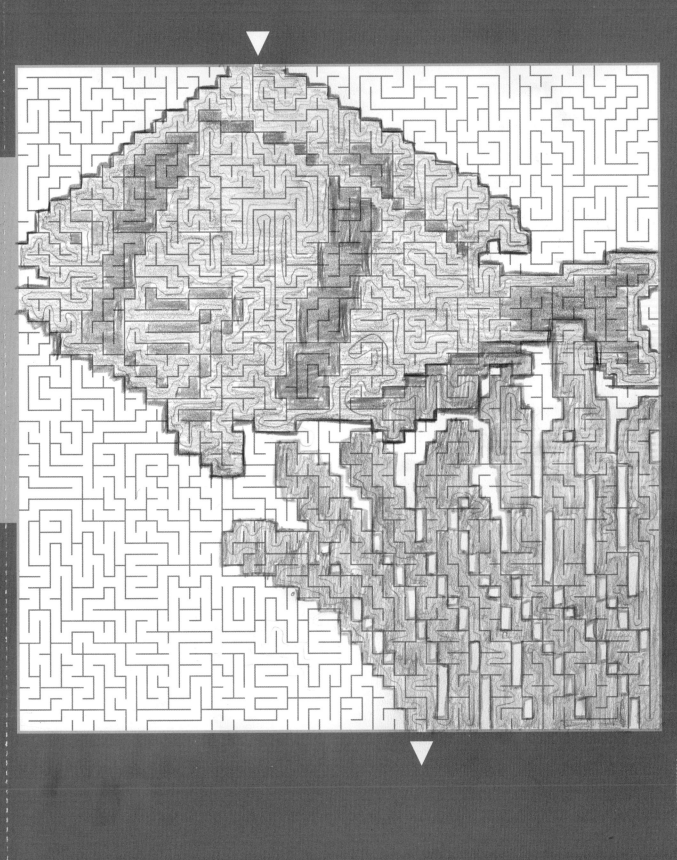

9

These insects are native to the midwestern prairies of the United States. They spend most of their life underground, using their large, flat front legs to dig elaborate tunnel systems. When it's time to mate, males will dig acoustic burrows—funnel-shaped tunnels that act like a megaphone to amplify the sound of their mating calls. They are the only insects known to do so and can be heard from more than 1,200 feet (over three football fields!) away.

Solution on page 111.

10

Solution on page 112.

There are 951 species of these nocturnal mammals, which vary greatly in size and diet. Some sip on flower nectar, others munch on fish or insects, and three species drink blood. But one trait they all share is that they're the only mammals with the ability to fly. They are famous for sleeping upside down, which is actually out of necessity, since many species' legs can't support their bodies. Females even give birth upside down, using their wings to catch their offspring as they fall.

11

There are roughly 2,000 species of this arachnid, a testament to their hardiness and adaptability. First appearing 430 million years ago, they have hardly changed, despite now living everywhere from deserts to rain forests.

They can drastically slow their metabolism—some species by two-thirds—allowing them to survive on less food. Some species have even been known to get by eating one insect in a year.

Solution on page 112.

12

Discovered from fossils dating back 400 million years, it was generally accepted that this fish had gone extinct with the dinosaurs more than 65 million years ago . . . until one was discovered in 1938 off the coast of South Africa.

The discovery provides insight into the transition of life from water to land: These fish give birth to live young, have four fins that move in the same way as the feet of most four-legged land animals, and are most closely related to lungfish.

Solution on page 112.

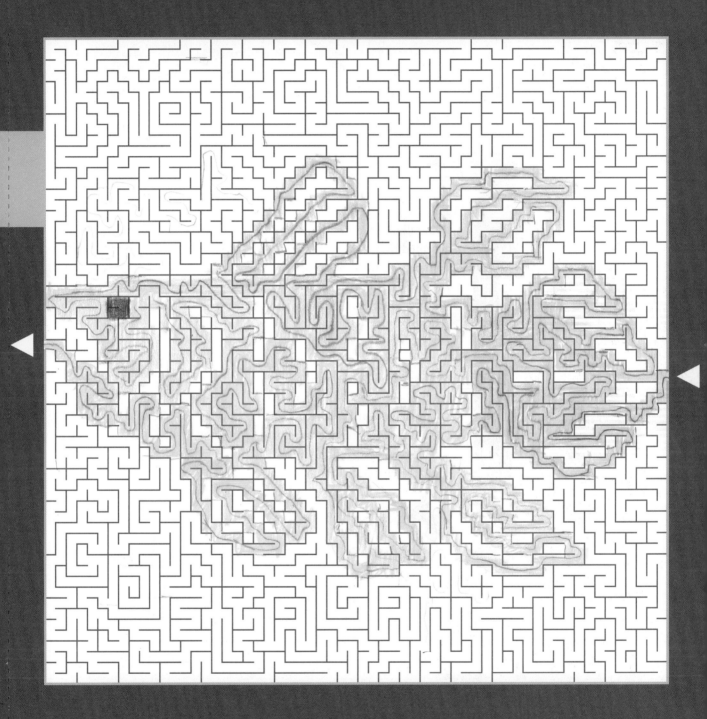

13

More people depend on this Asian mammal than any other domesticated animal. In fact, since they are so commonly used to plow rice paddies, they are sometimes affectionately known as the "living tractor of the East." They also provide a form of transportation, milk and meat for consumption, and dung that is used both for fertilizer and as fuel for fires.

Solution on page 112.

14

These animals are known for their long tusks, which can grow up to three feet long and are well suited to helping them live in the frigid waters near the Arctic Circle. Their wide-ranging uses include defense against predators (orcas and polar bears), making air holes by bashing through up to 7.9 inches of ice, and hooking onto ice to either keep them secure while sleeping or help leverage them out of water. This latter use is probably the reason for its scientific name, which is Greek and Scandinavian for "tooth-walking seahorse."

Solution on page 112.

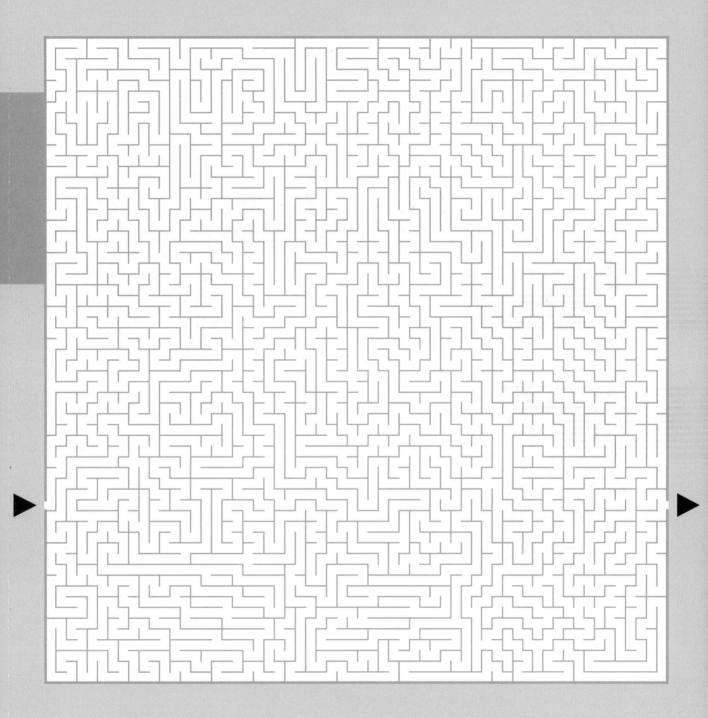

15

These birds spend their time wading in shallow waters across Europe, Asia, and Africa. They are visually striking, with white bodies and bold black patterns. Their upward-curving beaks help them scoop up crustaceans and insects. When trawling for food, they sweep their necks back and forth in a unique scything motion.

Solution on page 112.

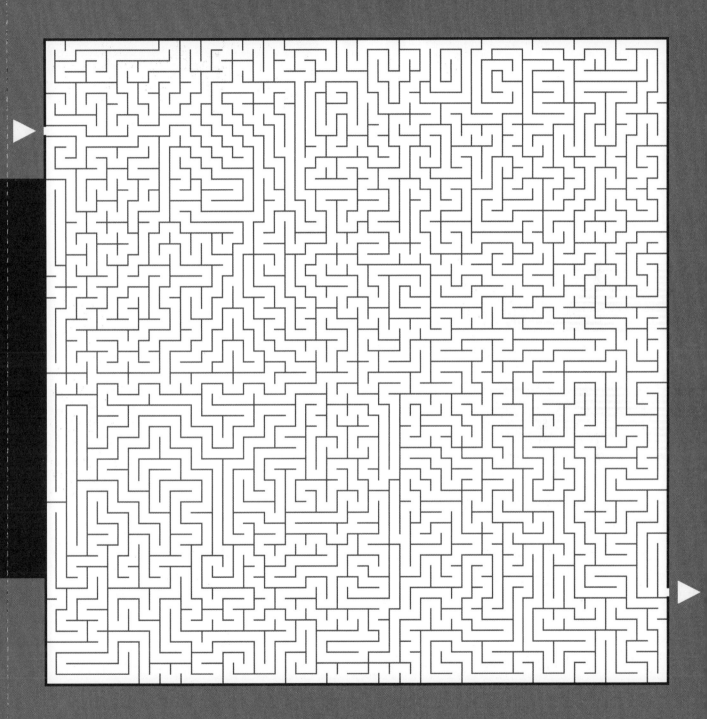

16

Ranging from about two to three inches in length in Southeast Asia, this is one of the largest insects in the world. A predator, it captures small fish and tadpoles and feeds on their body fluid. Found in ponds and rice paddies, it's even been known to capture carp and snakes! However, due to construction and chemical fertilizer runoff polluting their habitat, their numbers have significantly decreased and they are in danger of extinction.

Solution on page 112.

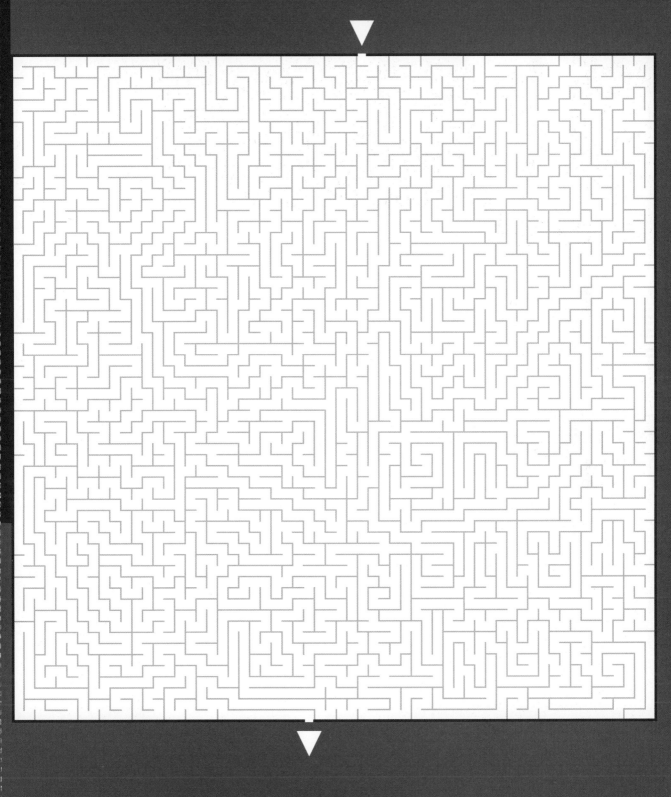

17

You are probably aware that humans' closest relatives are exceptionally smart, but are you also aware that they are experiencing their own Stone Age? They use a wide range of tools, from sticks to stone hammers, to find insects and open nuts. Leaves provide alternatives to hygienic napkins and toilet paper, and certain plants are used as medicine. They even use tools in different combinations or in succession as a primitive tool set. These animals also understand fairly advanced concepts like trading, cooperation, and deception. Beyond these adaptations, though, these animal groups have *culture*. Since knowledge is passed down across generations, different regions have created different tool kits. Combined with their various diets and expressions (think of it as being like human accents or dialects), they have developed some truly complex societies.

Solution on page 112.

18

This animal's name means "earth pig" in the South African language of Afrikaans. The "earth" part of their name refers to their talent for digging. In fact, with a rate of two feet every 15 seconds, they are one of the fastest-digging mammals in the world. The "pig" part of their name refers to their piglike snouts. But unlike the pig, they can actually close their nostrils— a trick that comes in handy when raiding termite and ant mounds for a midnight meal.

Solution on page 112.

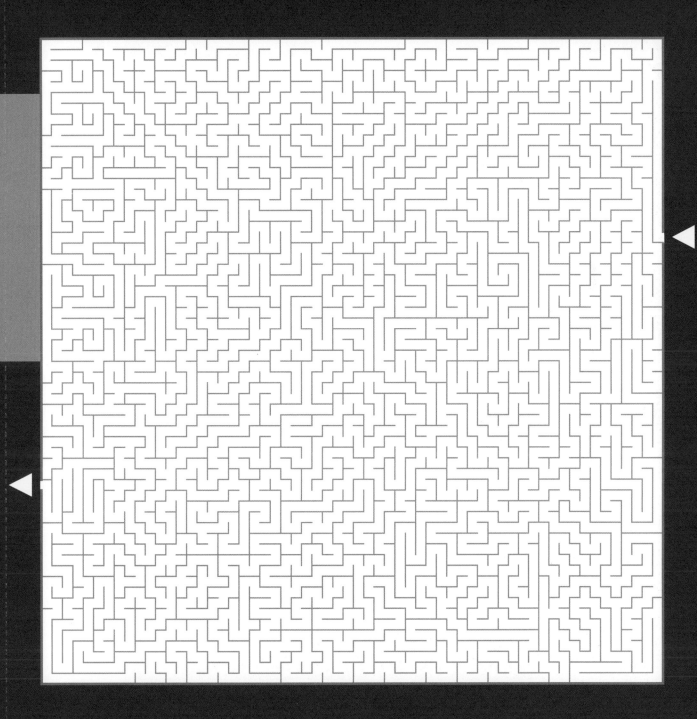

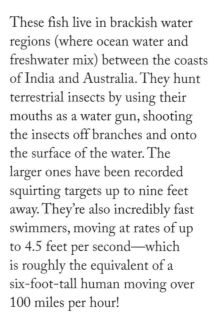

These fish live in brackish water regions (where ocean water and freshwater mix) between the coasts of India and Australia. They hunt terrestrial insects by using their mouths as a water gun, shooting the insects off branches and onto the surface of the water. The larger ones have been recorded squirting targets up to nine feet away. They're also incredibly fast swimmers, moving at rates of up to 4.5 feet per second—which is roughly the equivalent of a six-foot-tall human moving over 100 miles per hour!

Solution on page 113.

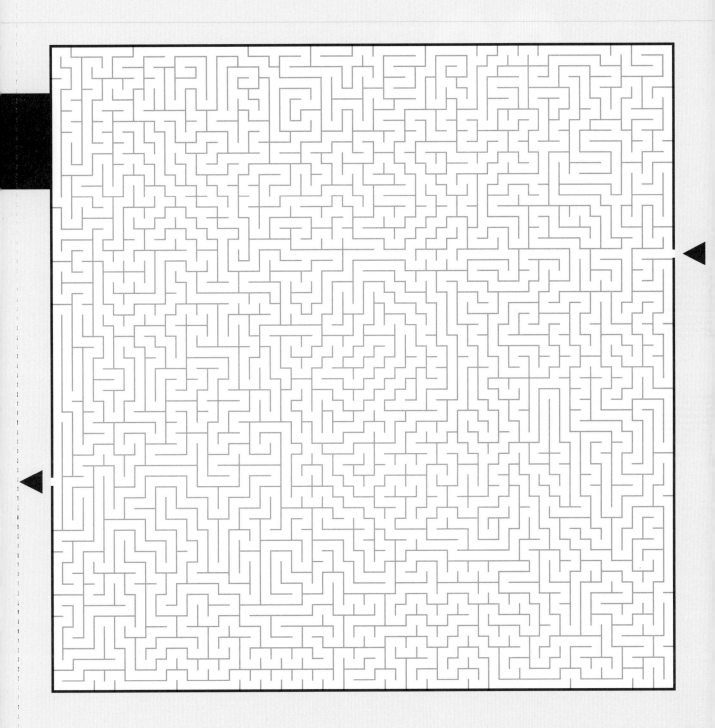

20

This endangered Japanese bird is being brought back from the brink of extinction thanks to extensive conservation efforts by China and Japan. At one time, they inhabited marshes and rice paddies in abundance. However, due to overhunting in the late 1800s and continued loss of habitat, by the early 2000s they were extinct everywhere except China. Successful breeding initiatives have led to the reintroduction of wild birds, and after many decades, Japan's special national treasure has returned home.

Solution on page 113.

21

Native to the forests of Central and South America, these animals spend 15 to 18 hours a day sleeping—which translates to somewhere between two-thirds and three-quarters of their lives! This is one of the adaptations required to conserve energy. Even when they are on the move, they top out at about 12 feet per minute. Put into human context, at a dead sprint they can complete one lap around a track roughly every two hours.

Solution on page 113.

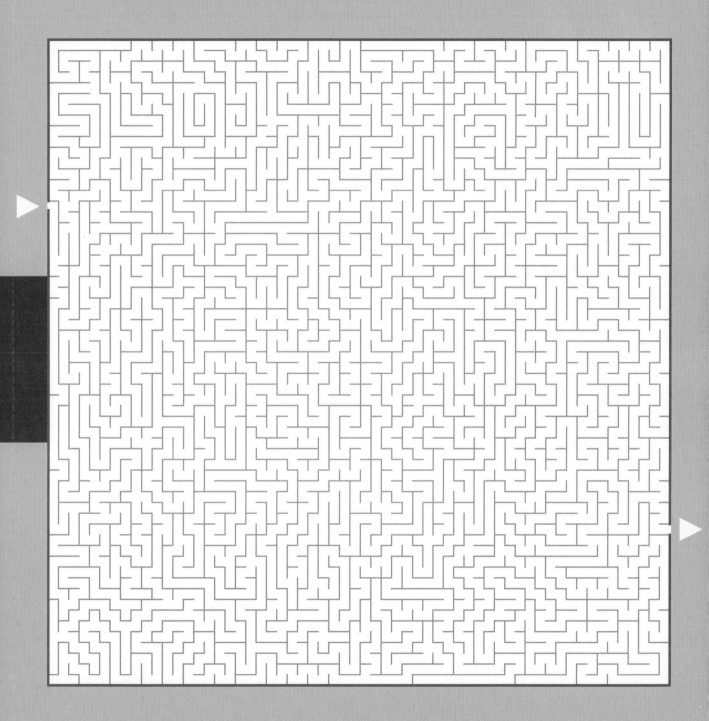

22

These fluffy, goatlike critters are native to the forested mountains of three Japanese islands. Because of this, and because they were once hunted almost to extinction, they are considered a special natural monument of Japan.

They are highly territorial and spend most of their lives alone in their home ranges. Boundaries are continually staked by scent. The scent comes from distinctive teardrop-shaped glands below their eyes, which look to some like big cartoonish tears.

Solution on page 113.

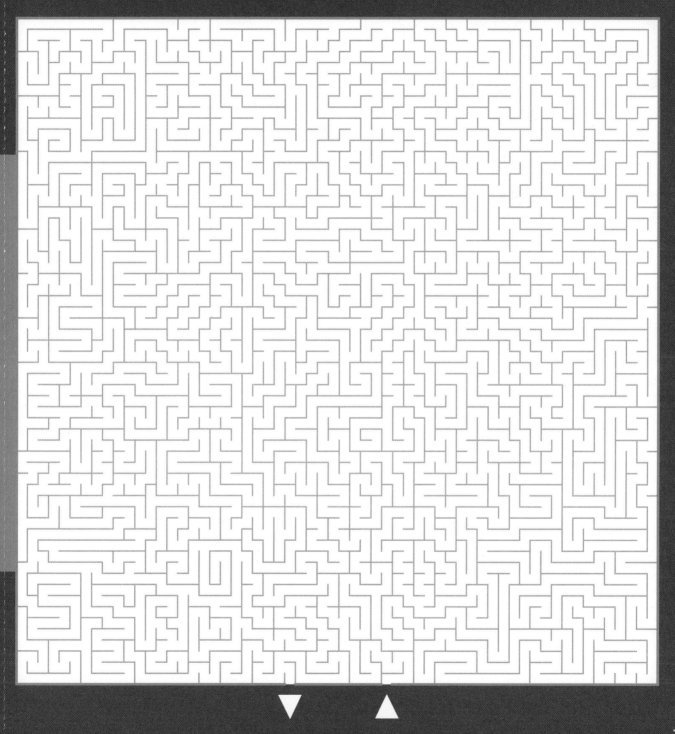

23

Native to the savannas of southern Africa, these mammals will migrate an astounding 990 miles in search of greener pastures. The herd consists of approximately 1.5 million members—plus hundreds of thousands of zebras, gazelles, and other animals— making it the largest mammalian migration in the world.

Solution on page 113.

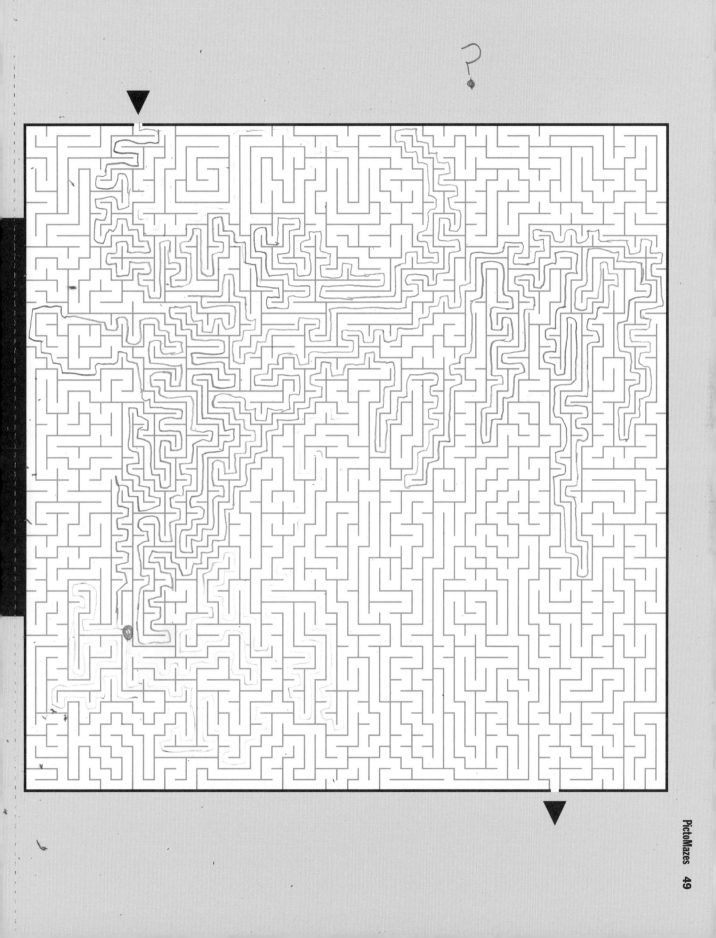

24

Wherever humans live, you can find this species. There are more than 40 breeds, in all shapes and sizes. And they're probably one of the first species you think of when you think of domesticated animals.

Recent evidence suggests, however, that these animals are only semidomesticated. If you compare their level of independence with that of dogs, and if you know that they've only been hanging around humans for 10,000 years compared to the dog's 40,000, this makes sense. So the next time you see one of these act independently, you'll know why.

Solution on page 113.

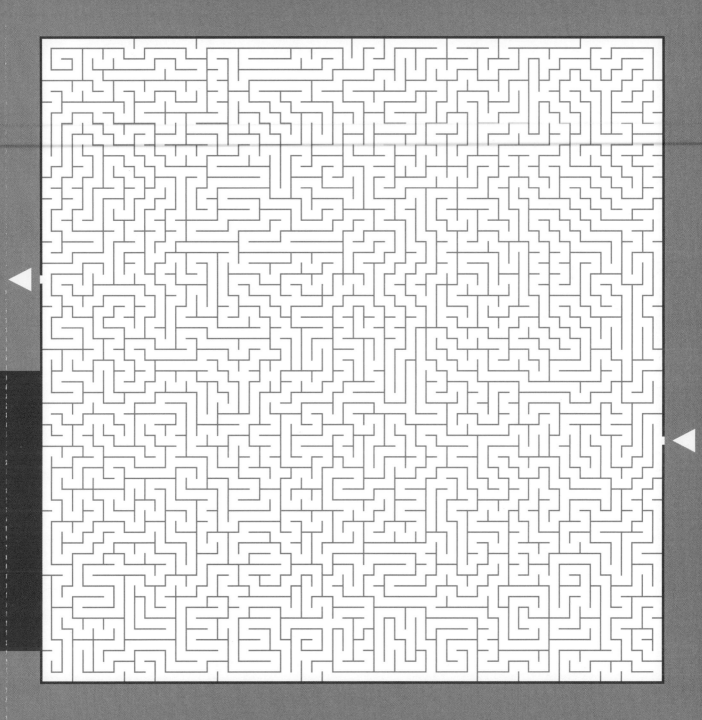

These saltwater fish are known for their long, toothed snouts—called rostrums—that look like the cutting edges of a chainsaw. Rostrums can be up to one-third of their total body length, or 18 inches long! They have whiskerlike sensory organs called barbels that sift through the ocean floor's silt for small fish and crustaceans. When they find their prey, they disable it with a sideways swipe of their rostrum.

Solution on page 113.

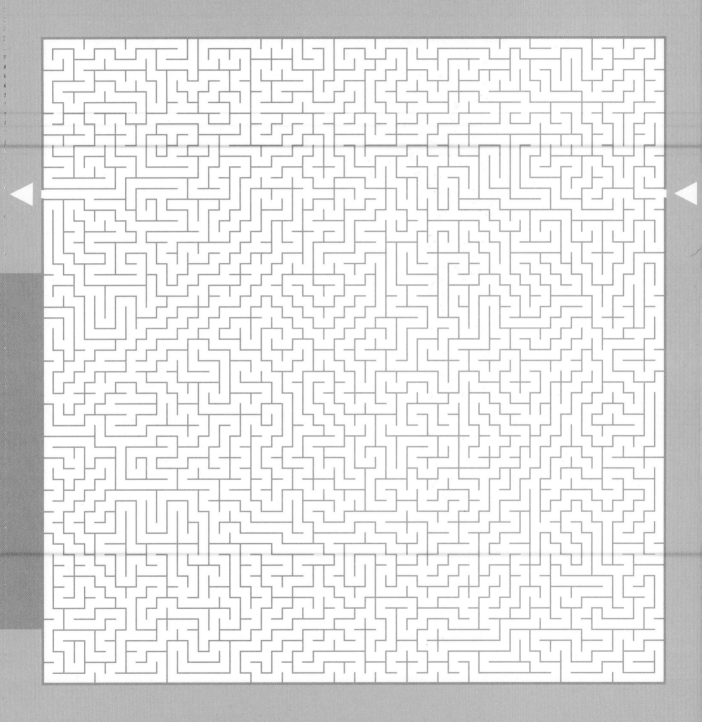

This bird is capable of mighty things with its tiny body. During a courtship display, where the male soars up to 150 feet in the air, plummets toward the female, and pulls out of the dive a mere two to three inches away, their wings can beat up to 200 times per *second*. The female, for her part, lays eggs that are a little less than half the length of her body. Both males and females migrate 5,000 miles every year; they have a resting heart rate of 480 beats per minute, and an elevated heart rate of 1,260 beats per minute.

Solution on page 113.

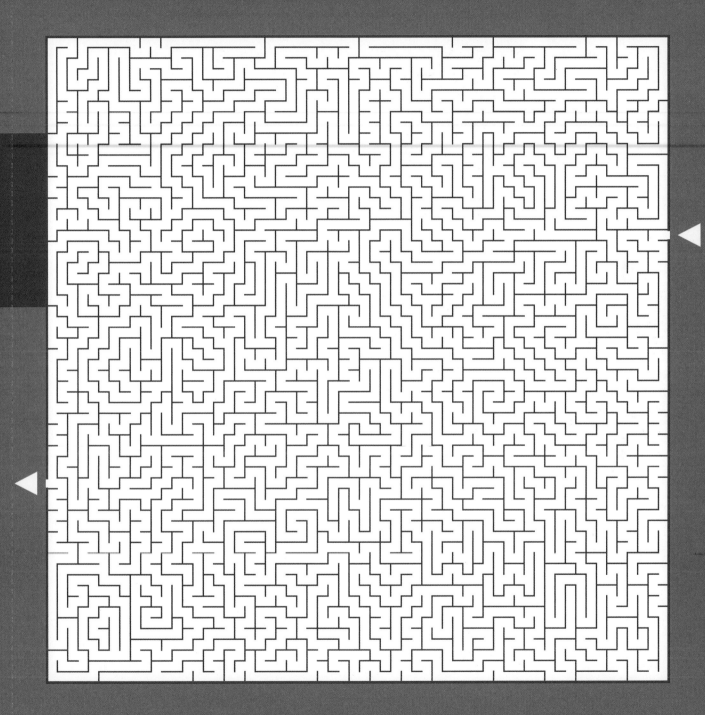

27

Endemic to the forests of the southern Philippines, this "flying" mammal is known for having a thin membrane, called a patagium, which connects at the neck, toes, and the tip of the tail. When the patagium is stretched out, the animal can glide from treetop to treetop, like a kite, for upward of 330 feet.

Solution on page 113.

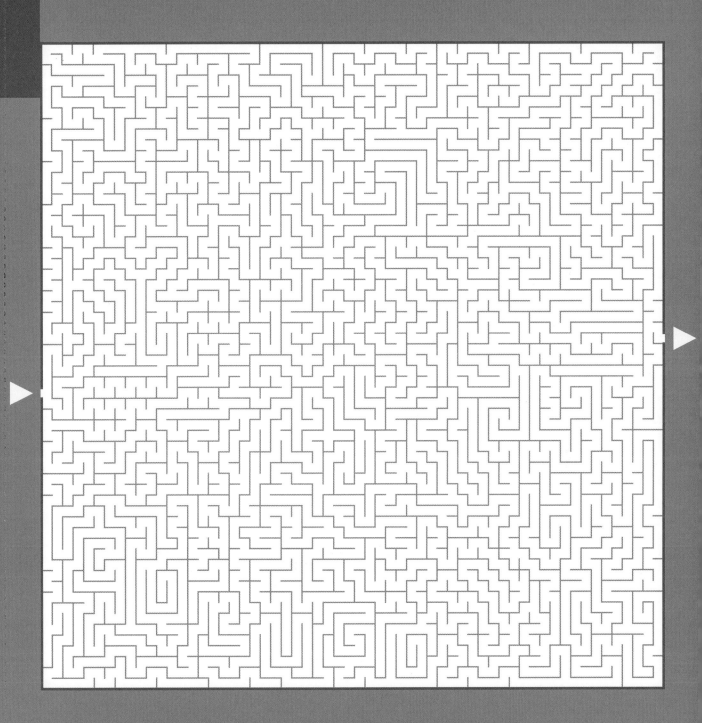

28

Their name is an old Spanish word for "flaming" or "red feather," which refers to their famously bright pinkish-orange color. They get this color from nutrients in the algae and crustaceans they eat; when deprived of these foods, their feathers grow in a very pale pink shade. Sun will cause the color to fade, so regular access to food in their standard diet is required for these animals to maintain their showy shades.

Solution on page 114.

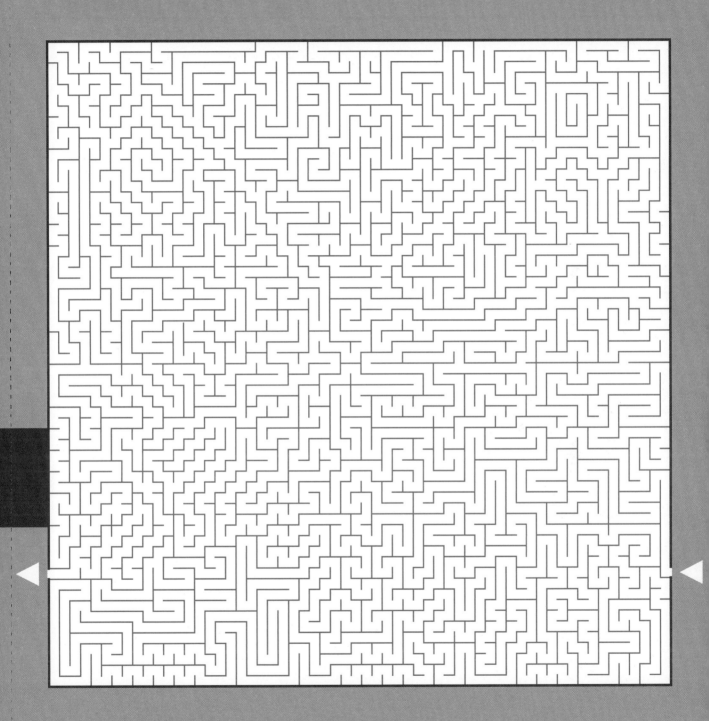

29

These are the tallest mammals in North America, reaching heights of 6.5 feet at the shoulder. Despite being large, however, they're quite agile. They are good swimmers, known to swim for multiple miles and to hold their breath for up to 30 seconds. They can sprint at up to 35 miles per hour for short distances and can trot along at 20 miles per hour for longer distances. Their offspring, at five days old, can already outrun a grown human!

Solution on page 114.

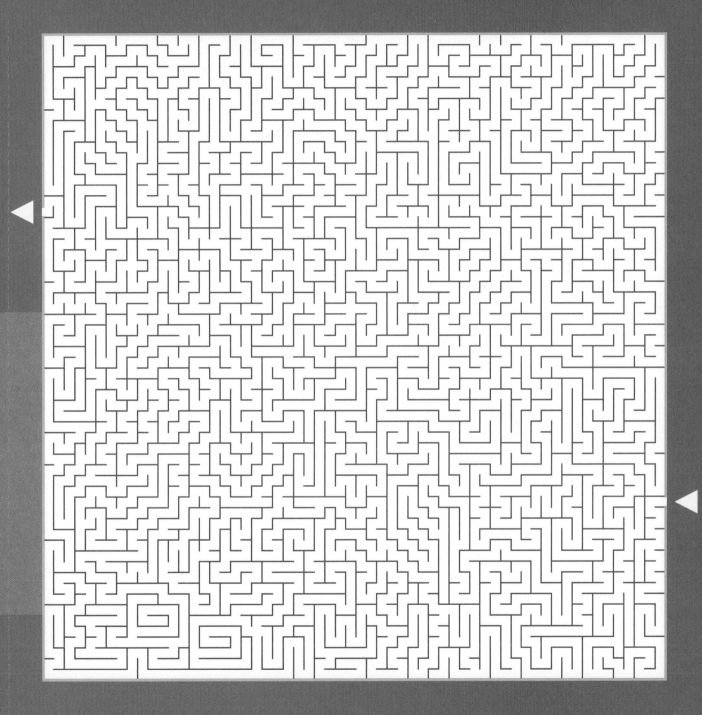

30

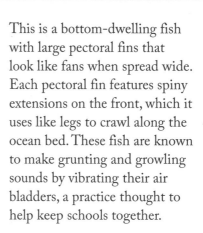

This is a bottom-dwelling fish with large pectoral fins that look like fans when spread wide. Each pectoral fin features spiny extensions on the front, which it uses like legs to crawl along the ocean bed. These fish are known to make grunting and growling sounds by vibrating their air bladders, a practice thought to help keep schools together.

Solution on page 114.

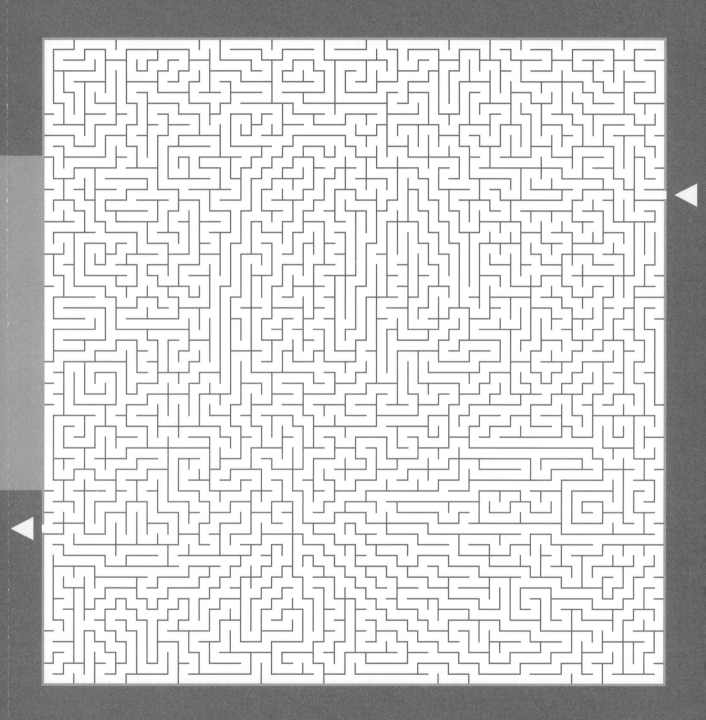

31

Monkeys are split into two categories: Old World (Africa and Asia) and New World (Central and South America). There are many differences between the two groups, and these Old World primates have many characteristics of the latter, including nongrasping tails, opposable thumbs, and primarily living on the ground.

Solution on page 114.

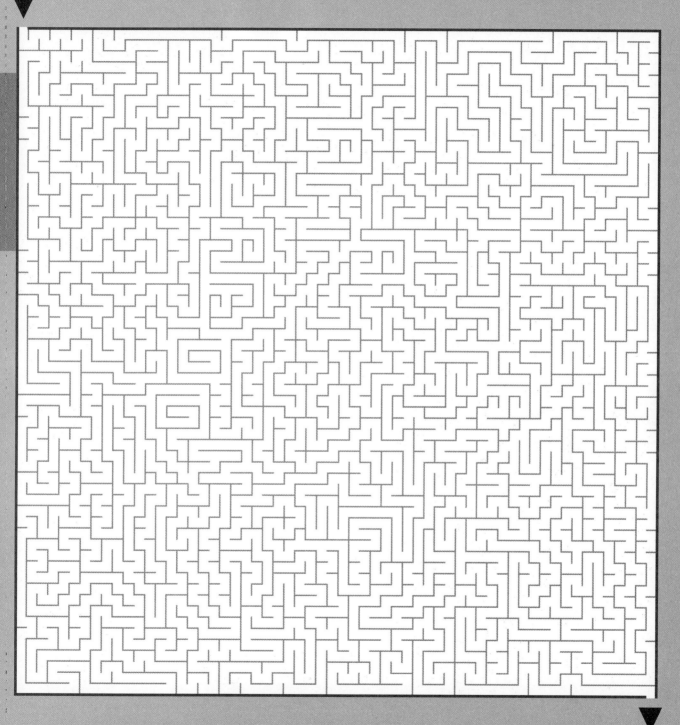

32

This formidable predator relies on its incredible hearing and has asymmetrical ears. Since one ear is slightly above the other, sound reaches one a fraction sooner than the other. The bird of prey then tilts and turns its head (which can rotate 270 degrees) until the sounds coordinate. Once the sounds overlap, the owl is facing the direction of its prey.

While these birds can hear 10 times better than humans, they still fly almost silently. While they lose some flying efficiency, the trade-off is that they are a nearly silent hunter—which helps as they continue to use sound to triangulate their target's location.

Solution on page 114.

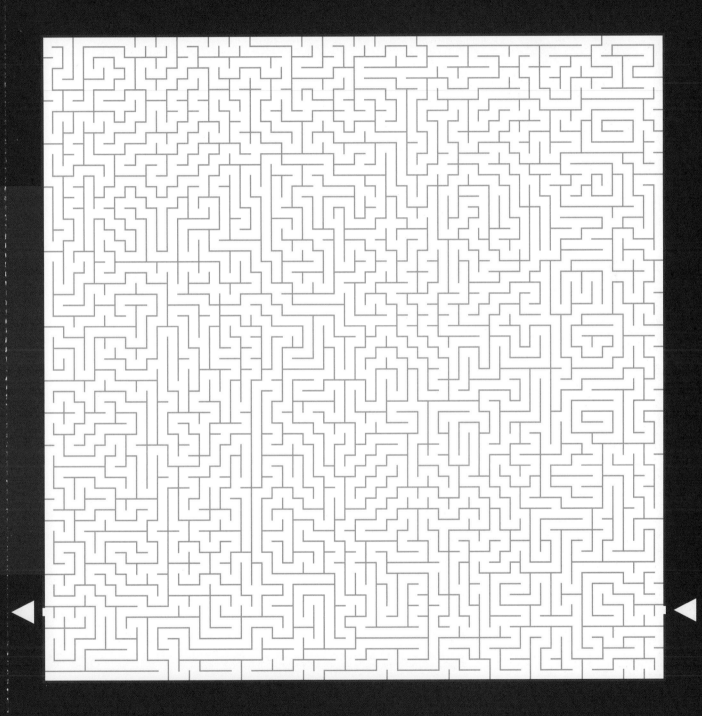

33

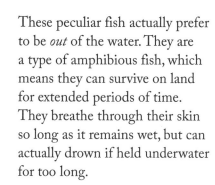

These peculiar fish actually prefer to be *out* of the water. They are a type of amphibious fish, which means they can survive on land for extended periods of time. They breathe through their skin so long as it remains wet, but can actually drown if held underwater for too long.

This leads them to prefer humid mud flats as habitats (they also happen to be faster on land than in water). Large gill chambers—which look like cheek pouches—hold water. These act as the fish's equivalent of scuba gear.

Solution on page 114.

34

These are some of the smallest primates, but proportionally they have the biggest eyes of any mammal. In fact, the weight of just one of their eyes exceeds that of their brain! The animals also hold the mammalian prize for having the largest infant size relative to its mother. Babies clock in at up to one-third the size of their mothers! They can leap six meters, or 40 times their body length—which is the equivalent of a six-foot-tall human leaping 240 feet (or two-thirds of a football field).

Solution on page 114.

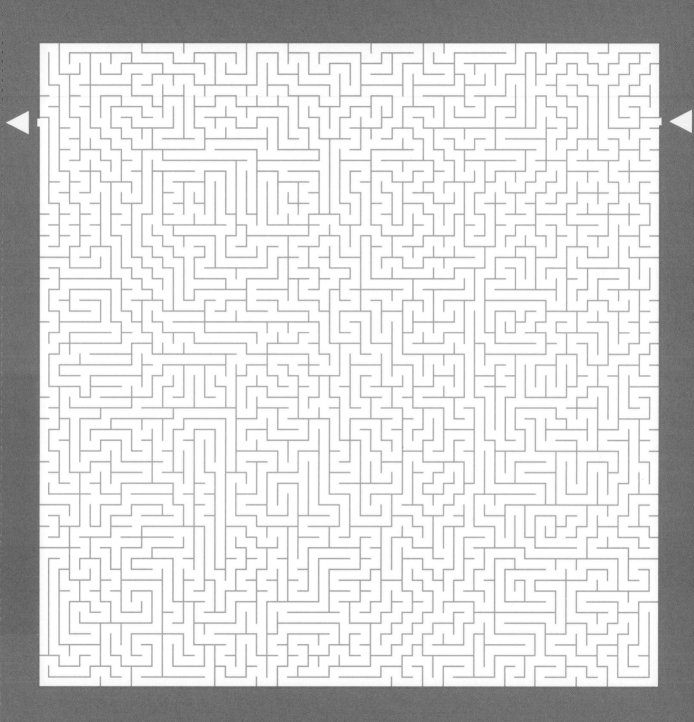

35

This small mammal is the smallest of its family, coming in at just over three inches in length. It is unusual among its genus for not living in burrows, instead using its digging ability to "swim" just under the surface of the scorching sand. (However, it does tunnel deeper during the hottest hours of the day.) Despite not having ears (or eyes) as we know them, it has a keen sense of hearing. Its entire head amplifies slight vibrations through the sand, allowing the animal to accurately target insects and lizards.

Solution on page 114.

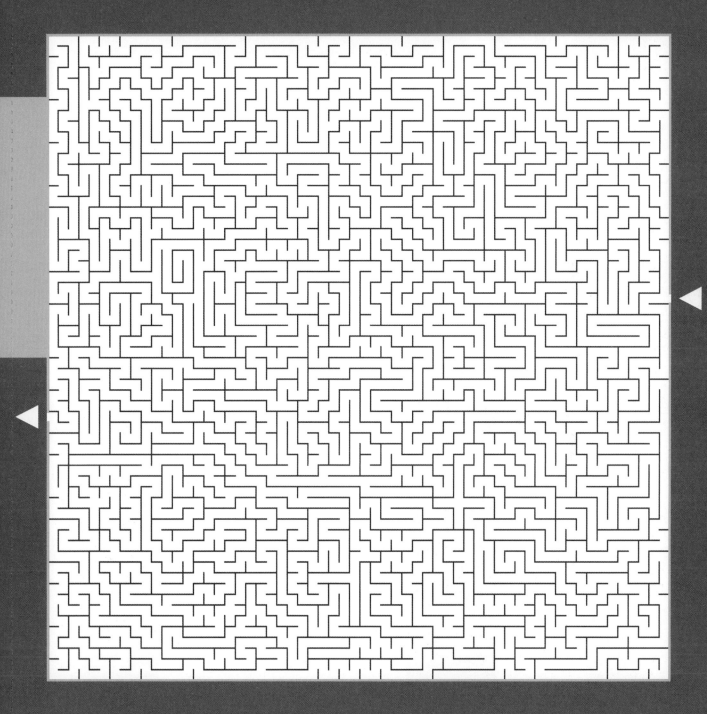

36

There are about 1,100 species of these crustaceans, split into two groups: those that live underwater and those that live on land. They all have soft bellies that they protect by wedging into discarded shells, and while most species use discarded sea snail shells, some species are known to make homes out of hollow pieces of wood or rock! As they grow, they will discard their shells and search for larger replacements.

Some species have been known to form shell exchange markets when a promising new shell opens up. The largest crustacean will switch to the new shell; its vacated shell is then inhabited by the second-largest, and so on until the smallest shell is discarded. This process is called a vacancy chain and is observed in other species as well, including clownfish with their anemones.

Solution on page 114.

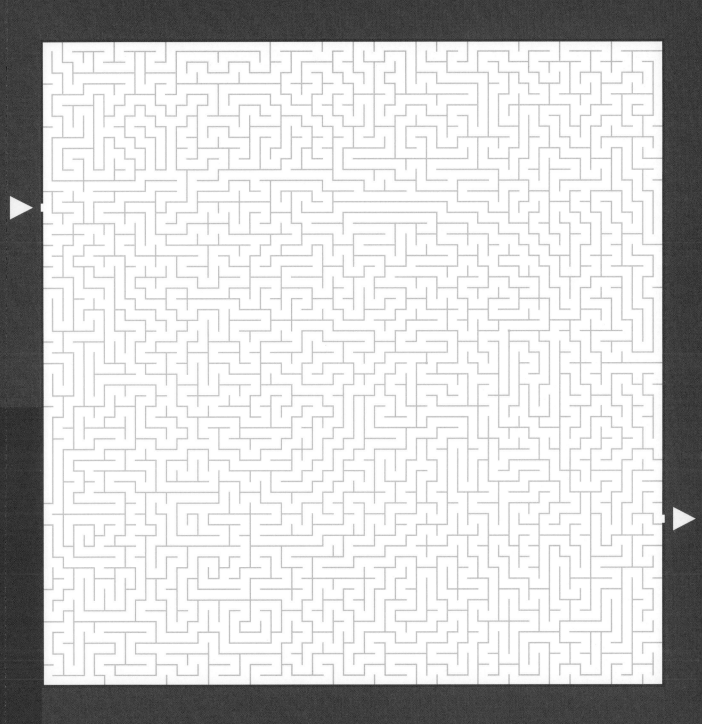

37

These dark-headed birds lose their distinctive markings in the winter, instead becoming white-headed.

They are uncommon in North America (instead inhabiting much of Europe and Asia) except in eastern Canada along the coast, but you would probably recognize their opportunistic eating and social personalities as characteristic of our own local breeds.

Solution on page 115.

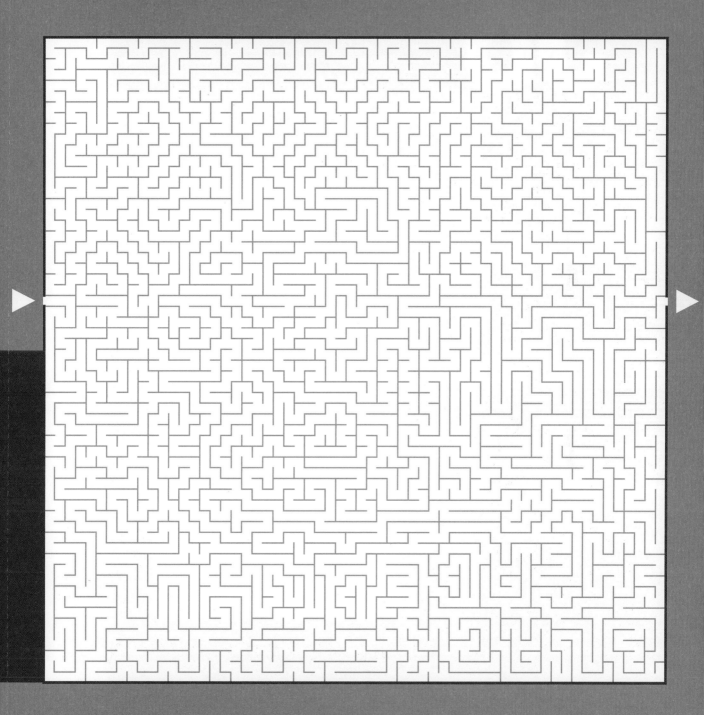

38

These are one of the biggest moths in the world. Females have a wingspan of up to *one foot* when fully open. And their wings are striking: The coloring and pattern are reminiscent of an ancient map, which is perhaps the inspiration behind their name. In Cantonese their name translates to "snake's-head moth," referring to the snakelike detail on the tips of their wings.

Despite their size, these moths do not eat (they don't have fully formed mouths) once they hatch from their chrysalis. As a result, they live only for two to three weeks in their winged form.

Solution on page 115.

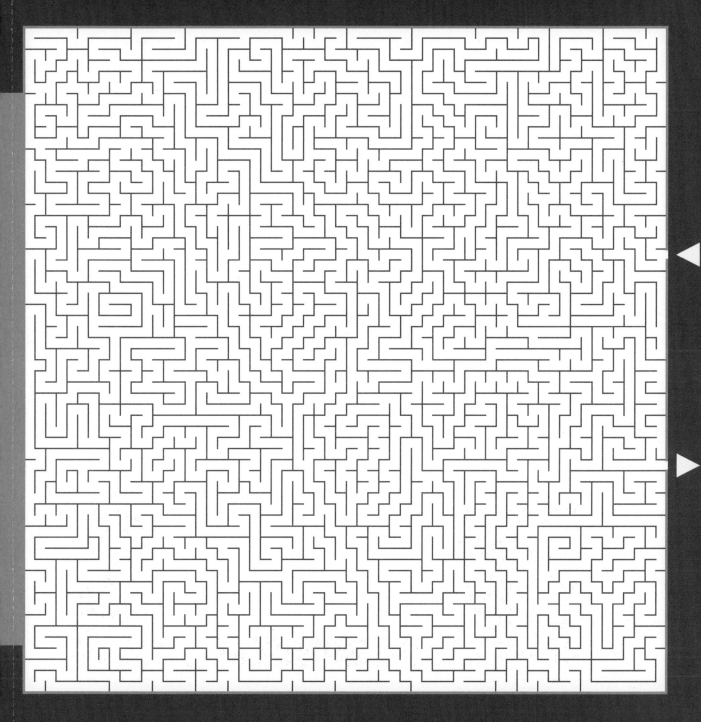

39

These animals, a member of the weasel family that lives in the ocean, are considered to be very clever: They put clams and crabs on their bellies and crack them open with stones. When they sleep, they wrap themselves in seaweed and hold hands so that they don't drift apart. They are also very playful creatures and have been known to devise games to play among themselves and with scuba divers. This trust is astonishing, given that they were once hunted almost to extinction for their fur. Their numbers have rebounded thanks to conservation efforts, though they are still considered endangered.

Solution on page 115.

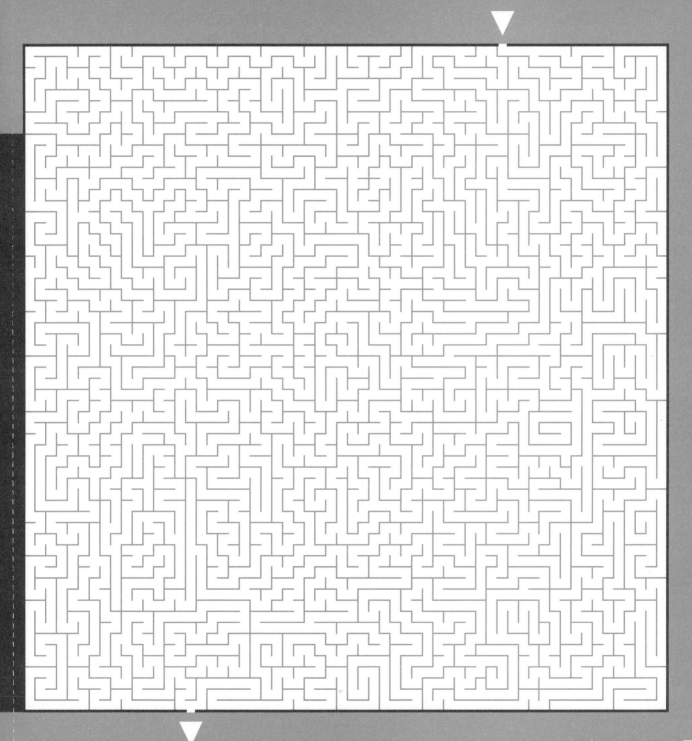

40

These canids live in packs averaging 2 to 27 members and are highly cooperative. As a cohesive unit, they raise their young; hunt; and care for elderly, wounded, and sick members. After a hunt, they will return to the pack and regurgitate food for the vulnerable in their family. Pack members are often closely related to one another, which may contribute to the noticeable lack of aggression between individuals.

Solution on page 115.

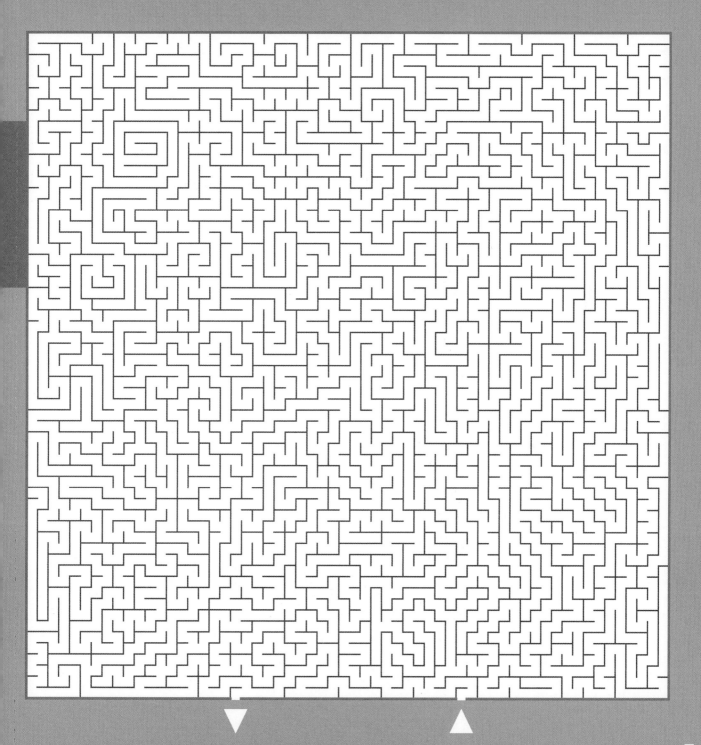

41

These beautiful and endangered birds are designated as a special natural treasure in Japan. They live in the forest of Japan's Oshima Island, where they feast on insects, small lizards, fruits, and even acorns. Their wings, tail, head, and chest are covered with deep purple-blue feathers, whereas their back and belly are a rusty orange color.

Solution on page 115.

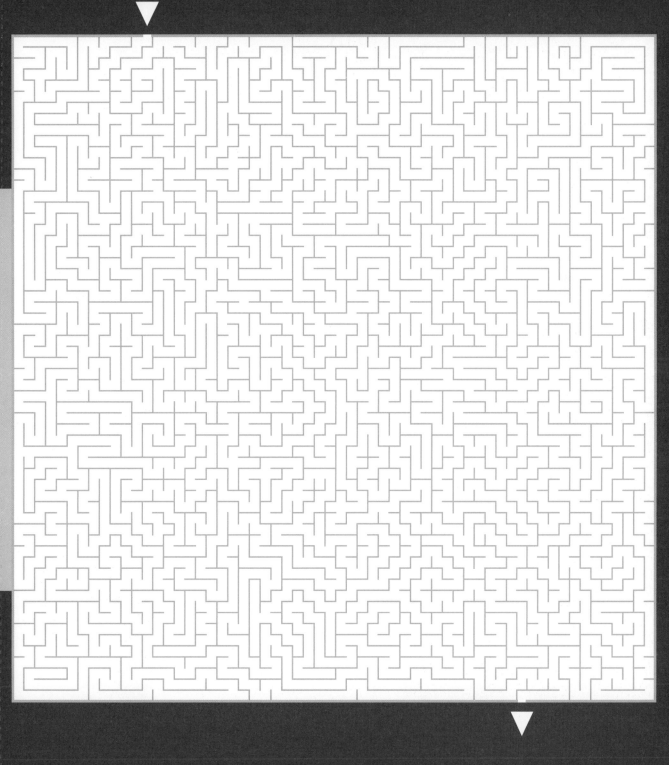

42

These mammals are considered living fossils, which means that, despite having a black-and-white "relative" with the same name, and despite their physical similarities to the raccoon, they are in a family all by themselves since all other species in that family went extinct three to four million years ago. Oddly enough, actual fossils dating back five million years have been found in North America, despite this species now living in small areas in the Himalayas at over 4,000 feet in elevation.

Their diet of bamboo gives them very little energy. They spend up to half their time foraging for food and have to eat 20 to 30 percent of their body weight every day. To conserve energy, they can reduce their metabolic rate to almost that of the sloth!

Solution on page 115.

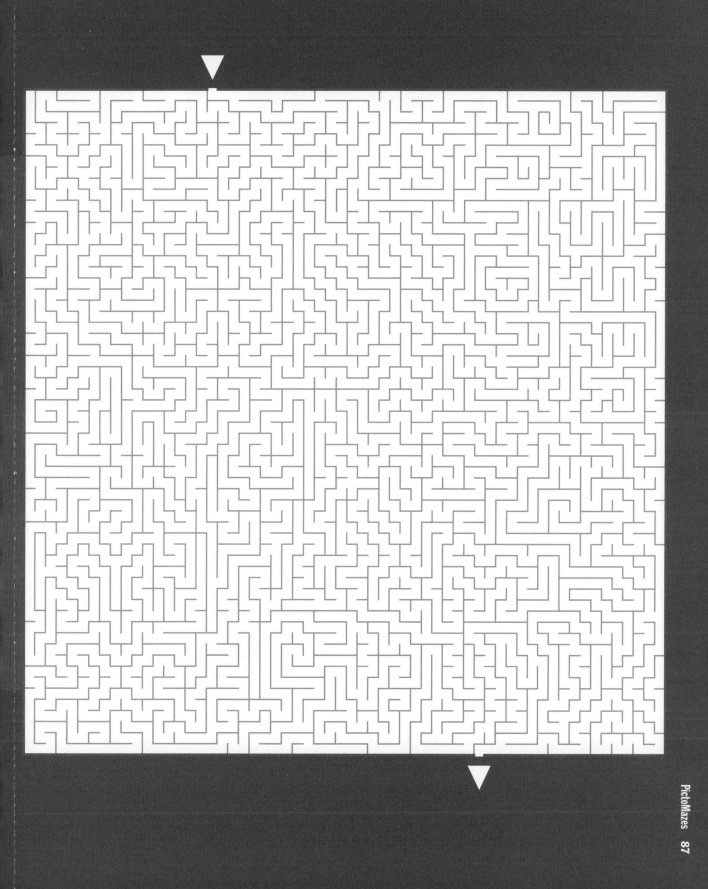

43

This crustacean continues to grow and molt annually throughout its life. Because of this—and because of its impressive lifespan—it can reach massive sizes. According to the *Guinness World Records* book, the largest one ever caught was 44.4 pounds, more than three feet long, and estimated to be at least 100 years old!

Solution on page 115.

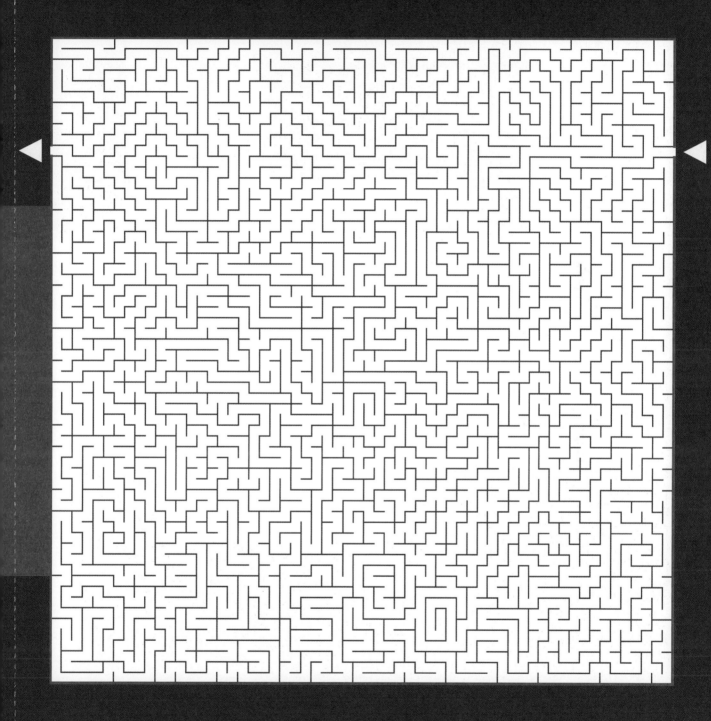

44

A few of the features that distinguish this animal from its relative, the alligator, are that they have a longer and thinner snout, are lighter in color, and have two teeth that are visible when their formidable jaws are closed. Can you find the distinguishing feature in the maze?

Solution on page 115.

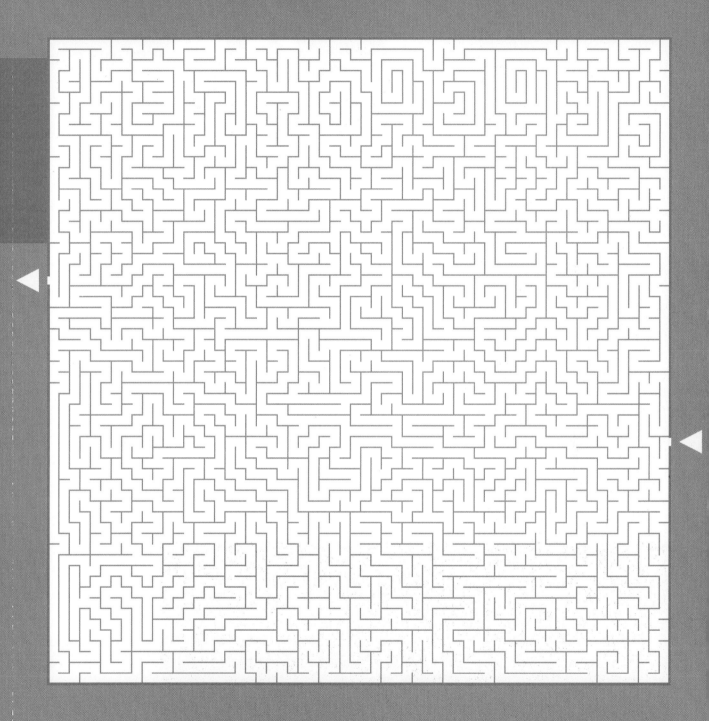

45

The largest wild cat in the world, this endangered animal is easily identified by its dark stripes. These stripes are as unique to each cat as fingerprints are to humans. This solitary animal hunts mostly at night, relying on sight and sound to stalk prey, and stays within its marked territory. It can eat up to 88 pounds of meat in one sitting! This animal is also a symbol of power in many cultures.

Solution on page 115.

46

Often incorrectly called the buffalo, this is the national mammal of the United States. While they are known for thundering across the Great Plains, their range was once much larger. Due to being hunted almost to the point of extinction, only 30,000 remain that are truly wild. The rest of the population has either been crossbred with cattle or semidomesticated by ranchers.

These animals are closely associated with the dams and homes—called lodges—that they build. Considering humans started farming only about 10,000 years ago, this mammal may well have beat us when it came to changing its environment to better suit its needs. Today, it is second only to humans in this field.

Solution on page 116.

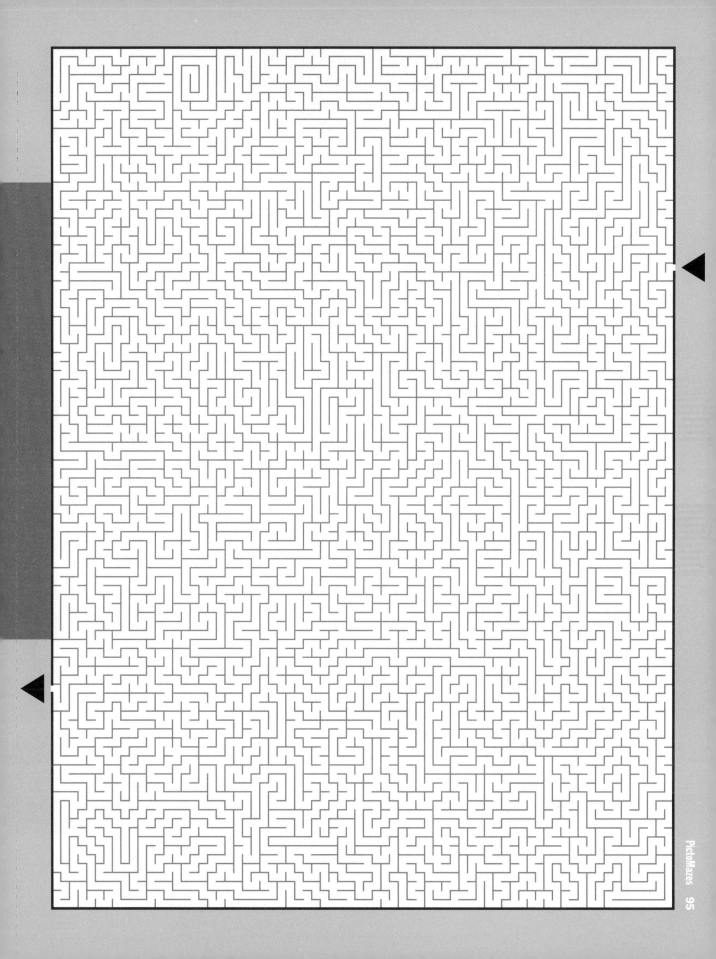

47

This Japanese crustacean is the most fished in the world, with 300,000 tons caught every year—so if you eat shellfish, it's likely you've enjoyed this species. They are the largest of their kind in the world that humans eat, reaching about 2.8 inches—though they have nothing on a relative which can grow up to thirteen feet.

These crustaceans, like other invertebrates, have a fluid known as hemolymph instead of blood. This liquid is blue, due to the presence of copper. (Human blood is red because of iron-rich hemoglobin.)

Solution on page 116.

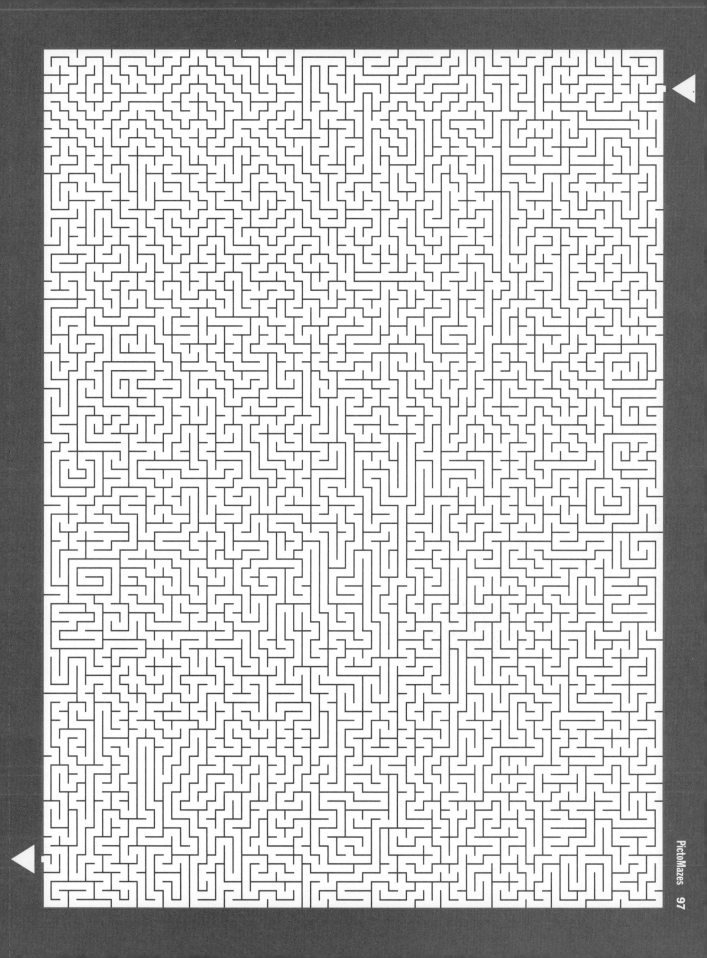

48

Male members of this species will "sing" for hours and can be heard for miles around, singing the most complex songs among animals. Scientists continue to work at decoding their language to figure out what they're communicating.

These animals are known colloquially as "cows of the sea." Their languid pace and grazing tendencies (they spend most of their time eating water grass, weeds, and algae) makes the comparison especially apt.

Solution on page 116.

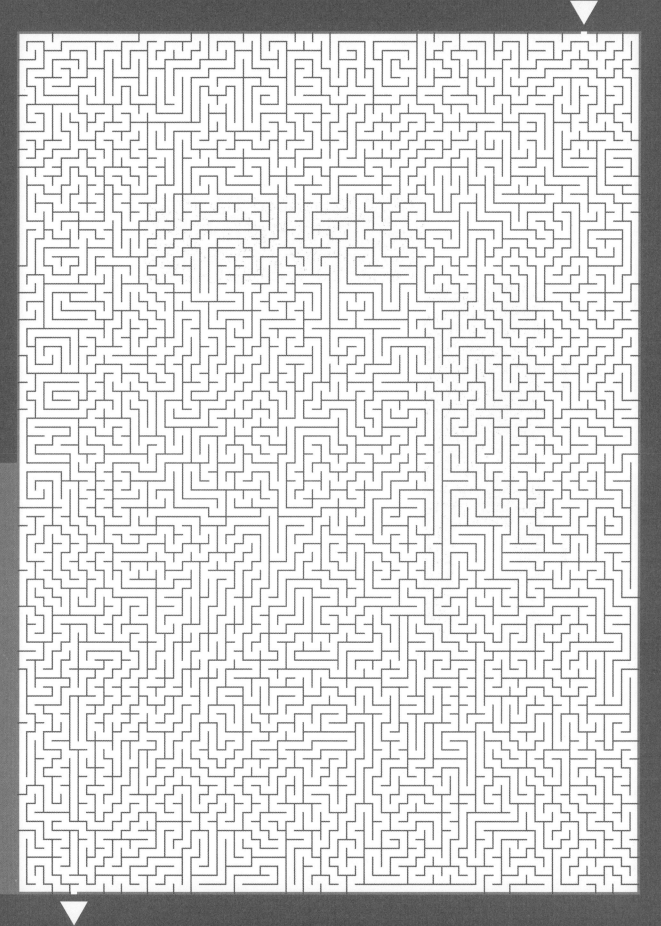

These fish are commonly kept as pets because of their flashy fins and vivid colors, but they're highly aggressive. They can be trained to do tricks, like following your finger or swimming through hoops.

This eel lives in coral reefs around the world. Unlike most fish, it doesn't have scales; instead it protects itself with a layer of mucus. Though it can look intimidating, tucked into crevices and flashing some wicked-looking teeth when it opens and closes its mouth, it's actually fairly docile, and the movement of its jaws is just a result of its breathing.

These fish possess a fearsome yet exaggerated reputation. Yes, they have striking teeth, but humans aren't generally part of their diet. In fact, some species don't eat any meat at all!

Solution on page 116.

50

The largest living birds on earth, they are flightless; instead they use their wings to balance their tall bodies as they zoom across sub-Saharan Africa at speeds of up to 43 miles per hour!

These birds are known for using their unusual beaks to catch fish. They'll scoop up big mouthfuls of water, which they'll then strain out, leaving only the fish behind. They will hunt in flocks, driving fish to shallower water and making it easier to swoop in and grab.

Their massive wings allow them to soar over the ocean for days on end, averaging 139 miles for each flight! To avoid landing—because they become waterlogged after a minute—they only eat flying fish.

Solution on page 117.

51

Named for the person who first bred this dog in Germany about 120 years ago, it is short-haired, possesses a dignified look, and has a state of high alertness. They are very loyal and don't get easily attached to people other than their families.

This canine has a distinctive face that some describe as "egg-shaped." At first, it was rough by nature, bred from terrier dogs to hunt vermin. Today, though, it is known to be charming and merry.

These are consistently one of America's most popular dog breeds. They are known for being great with children and are often described as "friendly" and "cheerful." As with all dogs, temperament, however, comes down to socialization and training.

This little firecracker of a canine is descended from larger sled dogs of Iceland. Queen Victoria was an early fan of the breed and helped popularize them the world over. The rest of their popularity can be attributed to their affectionate and playful nature.

Solution on page 117.

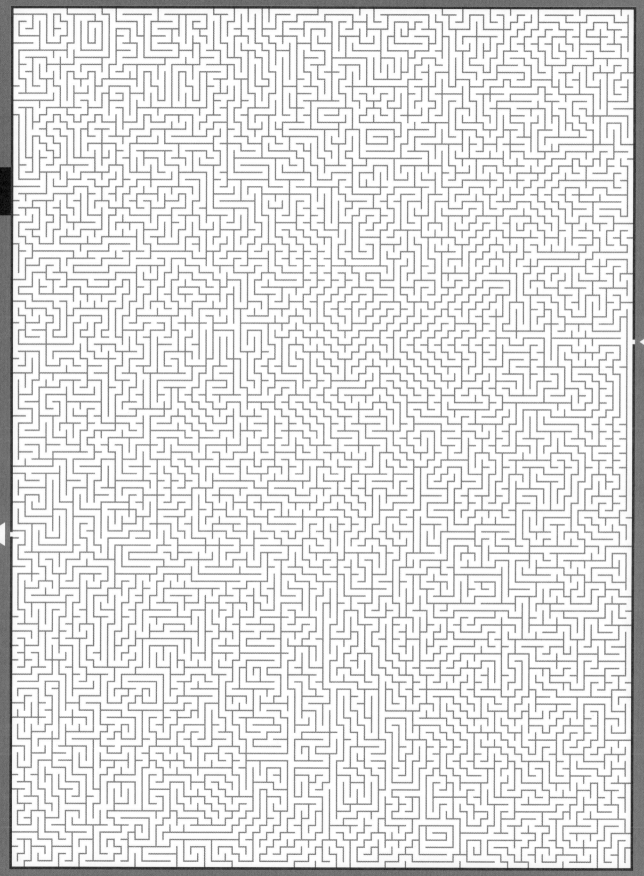

52

These large black-and-white butterflies can be found in wooded areas throughout Japan. Larvae grow by eating leaves of Chinese hackberry trees. In the adult stage, they gather tree sap from sawtooth oak and basket willow trees, but unlike many butterflies, they rarely visit flowers.

These beetles have a long mouth that looks like an elephant's trunk. Around the world they are largely considered pests because they voraciously eat food and other crops.

These beetles are well-adapted to the freshwater ponds and slow-moving streams they call home. To aid with their dives, these beetles breathe through spiracles located under their wings. When preparing to dive, they trap pockets of air with their wings to create their own air tanks!

At first look, this creature's wings appear to have a striking black-and-white pattern interspersed with splashes of jewel-toned colors. However, its wings are actually clear! Tiny scales cover the wings, and the light reflecting off them is what gives the appearance of color.

Solution on page 117.

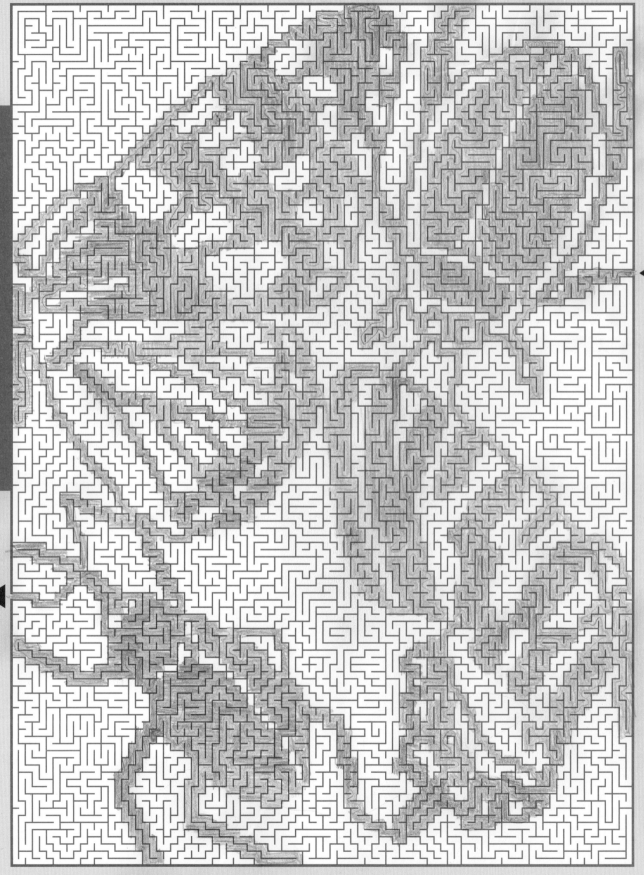

53

Considered to be a different creature from a dinosaur, these creatures could fly, but they probably conserved energy by soaring as much as possible—similar to the present-day frigate bird. Their large crests probably acted as a counterbalance to their massive beaks.

This dinosaur's most prominent feature was the giant crest on top of its head. This crest was made of two hollow tubes that connected to the nostrils, which scientists think allowed this animal to be able to produce noise—similar to an organ or a didgeridoo.

This small, carnivorous dinosaur found in America 140 million years ago had retractable claws located on its back legs. (One fossil's claw measured 4.7 inches in length!) It lifted the claws when it moved to keep them from becoming dull. One theory states that this dinosaur displayed early versions of feathers.

Solution on page 117.

Solutions

1

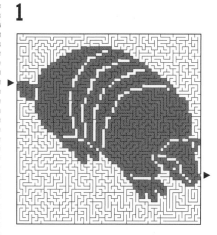

Southern Three-banded Armadillo
Tolypeutes matacus
page 5

2

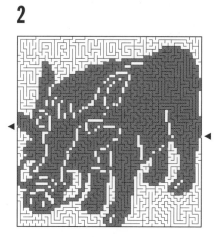

Common Warthog
Phacochoerus africanus
page 7

3

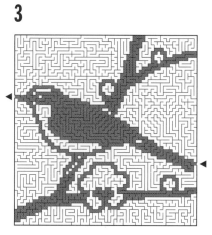

Japanese Bush Warbler
Horornis diphone
page 9

4

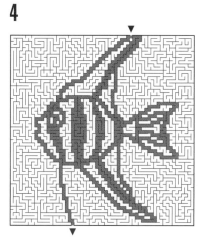

Angelfish
Pterophyllum scalare
page 11

5

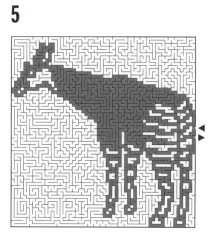

Okapi
Okapia johnstoni
page 13

6

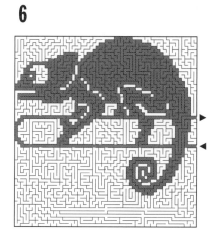

Tiger Chameleon
Archaius tigris
page 15

7

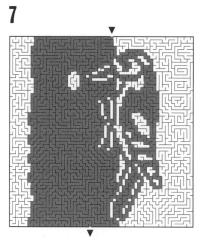

Amami Woodpecker
Dendrocopos owstoni
page 17

8

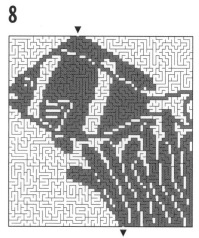

Clownfish
Amphiprion ocellaris
page 19

9

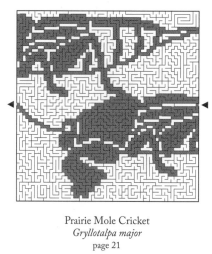

Prairie Mole Cricket
Gryllotalpa major
page 21

10

Bat
Taxonomic order: Chiroptera
page 23

11

Scorpion
Taxonomic order: Scorpiones
page 25

12

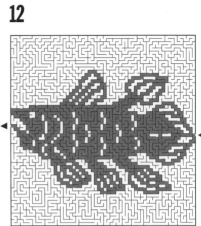

Ceolacanth
Latimeria chalumnae
page 27

13

Water Buffalo
Bubalus bubalis
page 29

14

Walrus
Odebenus rosmarus
page 31

15

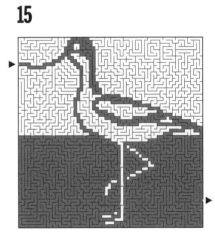

Pied Avocet
Recurvirostra avosetta
page 33

16

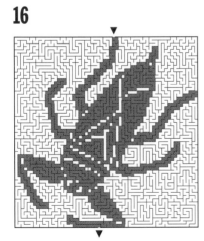

Giant Water Bug
Kirkaldyia deyrollei
page 35

17

Chimpanzee
Pan troglodytes
page 37

18

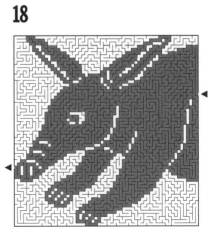

Aardvark
Orycteropus afer
page 39

19

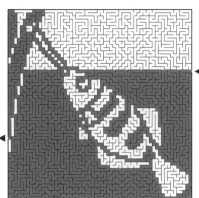

Banded Archerfish
Toxotes jaculatrix
page 41

20

Japanese Crested Ibis
Nipponia Nippon
page 43

21

Brown-throated Sloth
Bradypus variegatus
page 45

22

Japanese Serow
Capricornis crispus
page 47

23

Blue Wildebeest
Connochaetes taurinus
page 49

24

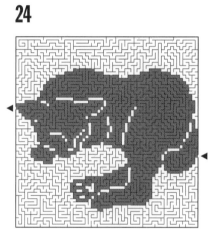

House Cat
Felis catus
page 51

25

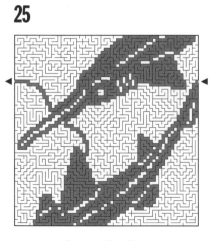

Common Saw Shark
Pristiophorus cirratus
page 53

26

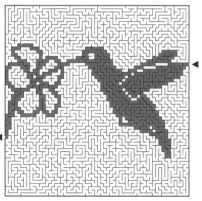

Rufous Hummingbird
Selasphorus rufus
page 55

27

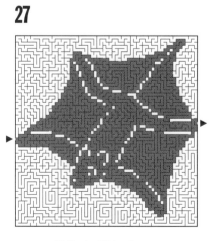

Philippine Flying Lemur
Cynocephalus Volans
page 57

28

American Flamingo
Phoenicopterus ruber
page 59

29

Moose
Alces alces
page 61

30

Tub Gurnard
Chelidonichthys lucerna
page 63

31

Hamadryas Baboon
Papio hamadryas
page 65

32

Great Horned Owl
Bubo virginianus
page 67

33

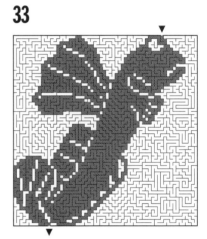

Atlantic Mudskipper
Periophthalmus barbarous
page 69

34

Spectral Tarsier
Tarsius tarsier
page 71

35

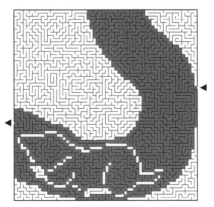

Grant's Golden Mole
Eremitalpa granti
page 73

36

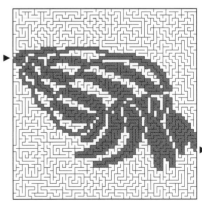

Hermit Crab
Taxonomic superfamily: Paguroidea
page 75

37

Black-headed Gull
Larus ridibundus
page 77

38

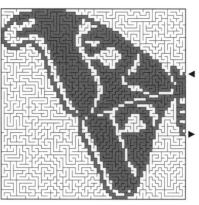

Atlas Moth
Attacus atlas
page 79

39

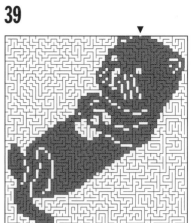

Sea Otter
Enhydra lutris
page 81

40

African Wild Dog
Lycaon pictus
page 83

41

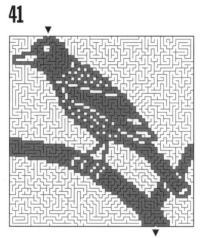

Amami Jay
Garrulus lidthi
page 85

42

Red Panda
Ailurus fulgens
page 87

43

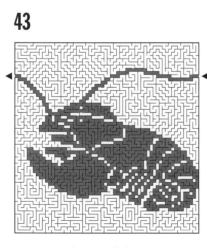

American Lobster
Homarus americanus
page 89

44

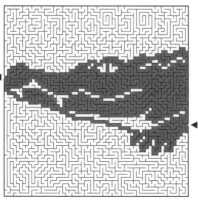

American Crocodile
Crocodylus acutus
page 91

45

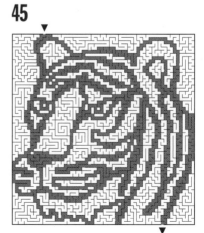

Tiger
Panthera Tigris
page 93

46

Bison (top), *Bison bison*
Beaver (bottom), *Castor Canadensis*
page 95

47

Japanese Blue Crab (left), *Portunus trituberculatus*
Snow Crab (right), *Chionoecetes opilio*
page 97

48

Humpback Whale (back), *Megaptera novaeangliae*
Manatee (front), *Trichechus manatus*
page 99

49

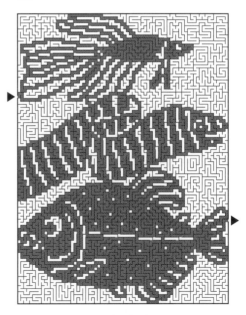

Siamese Fighting Fish (top), *Betta splendens*
Zebra Moray Eel (middle), *Gymnomuraena zebra*
Red-bellied Piranha (bottom), *Pygocentrus nattereri*
page 101

50

Ostrich (top), *Struthio camelus*
Great White Pelican (middle), *Pelecanus onocrotalus*
Magnificent Frigate Bird (bottom), *Fregata magnificens*
page 103

51

Doberman Pinscher (top left), *Canis lupus familiaris*
Bull Terrier (bottom left), *Canis lupus familiaris*
Boxer (top right), *Canis lupus familiaris*
Pomeranian (bottom right), *Canis lupus familiaris*
page 105

52

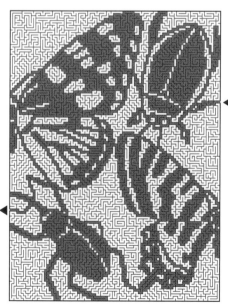

Japanese Circe (top left), *Hestina japonica*
Weevil (bottom left), Taxonomic superfamily: Curculionoidea
Diving Beetle (top right), *Dytiscus marginalis*
Japanese Luehdorfia (bottom right), *Luehdorfia japonica*
page 107

53

Pteranodon (top), *Pteranodon*
Parasaurolophus walkeri (middle), *Parasaurolophus walkeri*
Deinonychus antirrhopus (bottom), *Deinonychus antirrhopus*
page 109

About the Authors

 Nikoli Publishing, the premier Japanese puzzle and game company, holds the trademark on Sudoku in Japan, and supplies more than 300 puzzles to Japanese newspapers and magazines each month. In 2016, Nikoli produced MEGACROSS, a crossword with 66,666 clues. It holds the Guinness World Record for largest published crossword.

Kazuyuki Yuzawa (also known as "Mr. King of Mazes") works for an electronics manufacturer and has been handcrafting mazes in his spare time for more than 30 years. There are fewer than 300 puzzles created by him in the world.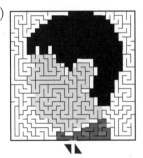